A NOTE TO PARENTS

When your children are ready to "step into reading," giving them the right books is as crucial as giving them the right food to eat. **Step into Reading Books** present exciting stories and information reinforced with lively, colorful illustrations that make learning to read fun, satisfying, and worthwhile. They are priced so that acquiring an entire library of them is affordable. And they are beginning readers with a difference—they're written on five levels.

Early Step into Reading Books are designed for brand-new readers with large type and only one or two lines of very simple text per page. **Step 1 Books** feature the same easy-to-read type as the **Early Step into Reading Books**, but with more words per page. **Step 2 Books** are both longer and slightly more difficult, while **Step 3 Books** introduce readers to paragraphs and fully developed plot lines. **Step 4 Books** offer exciting nonfiction for the increasingly independent reader.

The grade levels assigned to the five steps—preschool through kindergarten for the Early Books, preschool through grade 1 for Step 1, grades 1 through 3 for Step 2, grades 2 through 3 for Step 3, and grades 2 through 4 for Step 4—are intended only as guides. Some children move through all five steps very rapidly; others climb the steps over a period of several years. Either way, these books will help your child "step into reading" in style!

Library of Congress Cataloging-in-Publication Data
Mayer, Mercer.
No howling in the house / written by Erica Farber and J. R. Sansevere.
     p.   cm. — (Mercer Mayer's Critters of the night) (Step into reading. A step 2 book)
SUMMARY: Axel can't howl and Thistle can't fly, but they soon realize that there
are things they can do.
ISBN 0-679-87365-1 (trade) — 0-679-97365-6 (lib. bdg.)
[1. Monsters—Fiction.] I. Farber, Erica. II. Sansevere, John R.
III. Title IV. Series.
V. Series: Mayer, Mercer. Critters of the night.
PZ7.M462No 1996
[Fic]—dc20 95-13690

Printed in the United States of America   11 12 13 14 15 16 17 18 19 20
STEP INTO READING is a trademark of Random House, Inc.

A BIG TUNA TRADING COMPANY, LLC/J. R. SANSEVERE BOOK

Step into Reading™

Mercer Mayer's
CRITTERS OF THE NIGHT™

No Howling in the House

A Step 2 Book

Written by
Erica Farber
and J. R. Sansevere

Random House 🏠 New York

Wanda   Jack   Thistle   Axel

Bones

Snake

Capt. Short Bob   Dracul Duck   Wolf Mouse

Groad Frankengator Moose Mummy

Uncle Mole Zombie Mombie Auntie Bell

Meet the Howls.

The Howls live at Old Howl Hall.

Old Howl Hall is

on the edge of town

on the top of a very high hill.

One night when the moon was full,
Jack Howl took his son, Axel Howl,
to the top of an even higher hill.

"Now, son," said Jack Howl.

"The time has come . . ."

Jack Howl opened his mouth wide
and began to howl.

"Ahhhhh-ooooo!" he howled.

"Ahhhhh-ooooo! Ahhhhh-ooooo!"

"Now <u>you</u> howl," Jack said.

"All Howls howl.

It is what we do.

My father taught me.

Now I am teaching you!"

Axel Howl took
a deep breath.

He opened
his mouth wide.

And blew as hard
as he could.

But no howl came out.

"Try again," said Jack.

But no matter how hard he tried,

Axel Howl couldn't howl.

He couldn't howl at all.

On that very same night

at Old Howl Hall,

Wanda and Thistle stood by the stairs.

"Now, Thistle," said Wanda.

"Listen to me . . .

    "Birds and bats and bugs and bees,

    all that flies above the trees,

    rain and wind and sleet and snow,

    come to me—now up I go!"

Suddenly, Wanda flew up in the air.

Around and around she flew.

"Now you fly," said Wanda.

"All Howls fly.

It is what we do.

My mother taught me.

Now I am teaching you!"

Thistle closed her eyes
and said the spell.
But it didn't work.

She hopped

and skipped

and jumped.

She tried and tried.

But no matter what she did,

she couldn't fly.

She couldn't fly at all.

Later that night, Axel and Jack
came back from the hill.
And there, on the steps
of Old Howl Hall,
sat Wanda and Thistle.
"Thistle can't fly," Wanda said.
"Axel can't howl," Jack said.

Jack and Wanda shook their heads.
Then they climbed upstairs
and went to bed.

Axel and Thistle
kissed their parents good night.
They tucked them in bed
and turned out the light.

Axel and Thistle ran down the stairs.

Then they ran down the hall

to the very last door.

And there was Groad, the Howls' cook.

He was stirring some soup

and reading a book.

"We need a magic pie," Axel told Groad.

"What kind of magic pie?" asked Groad.

"A magic pie to make me howl

and Thistle fly," said Axel.

"To make that kind of magic pie,
we must go to the swamp,"
said Groad.

Axel and Thistle and Groad
went down to the swamp
with a great big pail.
"The first thing we need is the tail
of a swamp snail," said Groad.

"Then we need one cup of mud,
six pink bugs, and seven slugs."

"What else do we need

for our magic pie?" Thistle asked.

"The big toe of a purple toad,"

said Groad.

"There's a purple toad," Axel said.

"Shhh!" said Groad.

"Don't walk. Don't talk.

Just leave it to me.

I'll get that purple toad. You'll see!"

Groad took one step

toward the purple toad.

Suddenly, he stubbed his toe

and fell into the swamp!

The purple toad looked at Groad

and waved good-bye with his big toe.

"Oh, no!" Thistle said.

"There goes that purple toad."

"Without his toe we cannot make

the magic pie," said Axel.

"No! No!" said Groad.

"Leave it to me.

I'll get that purple toad.

You'll see."

Axel and Thistle followed Groad

to an old boathouse.

A purple boat was inside.

"On the count of three," said Groad,

"we will lift this purple boat.

Then we will put it in the swamp

and catch that purple toad."

"One . . . two . . . three . . ." said Groad.

Axel and Thistle and Groad

lifted the purple boat.

"Ow!" yelled Groad.

"The boat just fell on my big toe!"

Finally, they put the boat
in the swamp.

"Go after that purple toad!" said Groad.

Axel and Thistle rowed and rowed.

They tried to catch the purple toad.

"Go left!" yelled Groad.

"I mean, go right!"

Suddenly, there was a crash.

The boat smashed into a rock.

The purple toad hopped to shore.

"We'll have to set a trap," said Groad.

"A trap to catch that purple toad."

Groad set the trap for the purple toad.

The toad walked through the trap.

But the trap did not snap.

"What's wrong with that trap?"

Thistle asked.

Groad walked over to the trap.

Suddenly, the trap snapped.

"Ow!" yelled Groad.

"This trap has snapped
on my big toe!"

Axel and Thistle went home with Groad
so they could care for his big toe.
"Without the toe of the purple toad,"
Axel said,
"we cannot make the magic pie.
So I will never howl and
Thistle will never fly!"

"I'm so mad at that purple toad!"
Thistle said.

"Ahhhhh-ooooo! Ahhhhh-ooooo!"
she howled.

Jack and Wanda sat up in bed.

"Who is that howling?"

Jack Howl said.

"It must be Axel," said Wanda.

Wanda and Jack jumped out of bed

and ran down the stairs.

Jack patted Axel on the back.

"I knew you could do it, son," he said.

"But no howling in the house.

That's rule number one."

Just then Thistle howled again.

"Oh, my!" said Wanda.

"It's Thistle who is howling!

If Thistle can howl, can Axel fly?"

Axel said the magic spell.

"Birds and bats and bugs and bees,

all that flies above the trees,

rain and wind and sleet and snow,

come to me—now up I go!"

Suddenly, Axel flew up in the air.

He flew around and around.

"Ahhhhh-ooooo!" howled Thistle.

"Ahhhhh-ooooo! Ahhhhh-ooooo!"

"She howls like you,"
  Wanda said to Jack.
"And he flies like you,"
  Jack said to Wanda.
"What do you think of that?"
"I'll tell you what I think," said Groad.
"I'm going to catch that purple toad!"